Praise for *Pinion*

*Pinion*: The wing. To restrain by binding the arms. A gear. Within a single word—the title of this opulent collection—the inferences are packed like feathers around bone. Rico writes from the liminal exuberance between her hometown, "the constellation named Saginaw," a small industrial city which itself teeters on the edge of river, bay, and Great Lake, and México, "Michoacán to Michigan." Like Rivera's murals and Kahlo's paintings, Rico's poems exist in both allegory and the real. Her crows, owls, robins, and cardinals are real birds charged with the electricity of symbolism. The food she cooks and eats, edges singed by fire, so irrefutable I can feel the sting of lemon juice in the cuts on my hands, but also "[t]he taste of how / I got here," the brussels sprouts "[s]poonfuls of the green / crowns [her grandmother] once wore." Her father's factory work is "a landscape / of machines lit by spark," the engine block "a metal / heart...shaking a path through darkness." Throughout this majestic collection, wildness competes with entrapment. Her incorrigible hair drenched in oil and wrapped in plastic bags, her doll swathed in electrical tape. Beneath each feather, a knife. Within each brussels sprout, a crown.

Diane Seuss


Monica Rico is the poet we need now, and this book will be savored by all who read it—at this moment, and far into the future. Her work is charged with imagination, informed by experience. She combines the exotic with the familiar, bringing to each line the haunting music she hears, and to each image something beautiful and new, inviting the reader to see the world and all things in it through her entirely original eyes. This poet's talent arrives to us seeming miraculous, effortless, and fully formed. A remarkable collection, this is poetry that is essential, powerful, and unforgettable.

Laura Kasischke

# Pinion

# Pinion

## Monica Rico

Four Way Books
Tribeca

*For Todd Everett—for keeping me alive*

Library of Congress Cataloging-in-Publication Data

Names: Rico, Monica (Poet), author.
Title: Pinion / Monica Rico.
Description: New York : Four Way Books, 2024. | Summary: "Pinion, Monica
Rico Four Way Books 2024"-- Provided by publisher.
Identifiers: LCCN 2023031714 (print) | LCCN 2023031715 (ebook) | ISBN
9781954245907 (trade paperback) | ISBN 9781954245914 (ebook)
Subjects: LCGFT: Poetry.
Classification: LCC PS3618.I3835 P56 2024 (print) | LCC PS3618.I3835
(ebook) | DDC 811/.6--dc23/eng/20230816
LC record available at https://lccn.loc.gov/2023031714
LC ebook record available at https://lccn.loc.gov/2023031715


This book is manufactured in the United States of America
and printed on acid-free paper.

Funding for this book was provided in part by a generous donation
in memory of John J. Wilson.

This publication is made possible with public funds
from the New York State Council on the Arts, a state agency.

We are a proud member of the Community of Literary Magazines and Presses.

*Contents*

*Notes*

"If she put her ear up to the line after each engine passed her station, she could hear a faint chirp."
—Lolita Hernandez, *Autopsy of an Engine*

# An Unusual Bird Divides the Sky

I return, unlike the gray
    crow who has been
        missing for months.
I hope he has migrated
    to México with the
        monarchs and robins, not transitioned
to the holy blue spruce
    made of nebulae
        and squirrel chatter. My mother
tugs my shirt
    snug, no comment. I leave my
        shoes behind like banana peels. I
step into the kitchen because I can
    no longer smell the lilac
        bush my father cut down.
My mother tries to say *beautiful*
    but won't. She
        is busy trying to find
her favorite pan. She knows
    she does not
        have enough rice to feed
me and
    what about her coffee pot? The
        one I've spent

my whole life

      washing. I drink so much coffee

          it comes back to me

like the male

      house finch who lands in

          the cup of my ear,

flaps his feathers

      and hangs a mailbox from

          my earlobe. At least

I am alive.

      At what height can

          I find the gray crow?

The plum trees

      I drape my body

          from because they are

easy to climb.

      Among the crabapple and pear trees,

          a carpet of rotten fruit

no one tries to

      keep up with.

          Their sugar

emerges from my body

      like pressing puffy taco

          dough into seams

held together

      with a toothpick, they shimmer in fevered

           oil. I am told to look for

atomic number ten. A rabbit.

      The word frijoles, I eat.

         My father removes his

pistola from the ankle

      of his boot.

         A speck of sparkle that

bends into a shock wave

      swallowing outer space. I know a gray crow

         when I see one.

I return to the constellation named Saginaw.

# Mise En Place

I believe my father assembled me
from wings and duct tape. My mother said
he fell asleep and the next day I was born.
She didn't stop me

from planting avocado pits,
only from handling
a sparrow that fell from its nest.

Birds are mean by nature.

I grip the tail of a salmon,
knife between skin and meat,
I pull.

I never delighted
in the way men looked at my mother.
It's easy for a man

to find someone to wash his clothes.

A tomato loves a sharp knife,
light, and the sting of salt.
When I come home

she wants to know if I'm hungry.

I sit at the head of the table,
my husband brings me another fish.

# Heartbeat and Humidity

And
so
what
of
this
kiss?

This heat
more noise
than splash
through each
splayed feather
of the swan.
Is there
a necessary

difference between
heartbeat
and humidity?
The predictable
human body
easily missed,
as motionless as
a great blue heron,

stick of a bird.
In the middle of the road

a snapping turtle
forgot where it was,
waited for an interruption
asleep in a box made for a ring.
The crabapple
flowers prefer not

to suffocate
their bees
unlike Paris
when he snatched
the most beautiful woman,
she need

not be asked
what scent
veiled in loose hair
swept around the neck
ought to be cut
even if it grows back.
It is a trick,

if there is
enough
to pull
upright
like the neck
of a swan.

# Stolen and Unnamed

When my grandma died
her sister brought México
in her pocket

a bag full of dirt
and sand the chickens
hadn't run over
too much

small handfuls
of home
gunpowder residue
from the pistol she
slept with
beneath a pillow.

I was there to hear the voices
chanting as if on a train

towards México, handkerchiefs
like doves resting and wrapped
in worn rosaries who remember
the last time they saw their sister
young. *¡Qué bonita San Luis Potosí!*

No permission given
to her cousin
a thief and a husband.

Michoacán to Michigan where her
eyes became bullets or tulips
in the one photo I have

those same eyes I did not address
as abuela, too scared to lean in for one kiss,
a shiny blood line hidden in my throat

when she laughed and said,
I needed to be tamed, stolen,
and unnamed to taste this food.

# Cutting the Tail

The first of the line
      is tied to a tree and the last
        is being eaten by ants.
    The world must be
           all fucked up. It rained for four years,
eleven months, and two days.

I know all of this by heart.

        The yellow butterflies
          invade the house

and in order to indicate them
        it was necessary to point

       to be sure
          you     and I
     exist.

From now on        everyone will know    who you are,
    as if the world
        were repeating itself. It's enough
          for me

to be sure

        a person doesn't die

when he should      but when he can.

# On the Eve of the 2017 Presidential Inauguration

I turn bread into tortillas, and leave
dried guajillo chiles in my wake.
My hair is cilantro. My footprints are poinsettias.
My tongue is an eagle whose wings will shout.
The fringe of my rebozo is made of infinite braids

I dare you to touch. I am a field.
My hands are dirt, my fingernails are roots,
Diego Rivera has painted them.
My bones are made of corn and chiles.
My stomach is arroz con frijoles.
My lungs are comino y canela.
My blood is lemon and salt.
In my fingerprints are the spines of nopal.
Each one of my feet has six strings,
my steps are canciones,

ground down cigars and ash.
La Llorona leads my mariachi band.
¡Toca la guitarra!
I paint streets the color of mangoes.
My face is all skull and a halo of carnations,
My elbows are molcajetes ready to grind and smash any fool
who tries to build a wall around me.

Watch it crack like a tostada.

My shoulders are black doves.

My eyes are Última's owl, bless us.

My comal will save.

Say my name.

Say La Raza!

We will sing until we raise hell.

¡Otra más!

As Emiliano Zapata chose to stand,

we stand.

¡Vamos!

The Statue of Liberty has stepped aside

for nuestra Señora de Guadalupe.

From Her robe fall no tears, only roses.

The crescent moon offers enough light for us to be on our feet

among the stars,

among the holy,

among the mole.


We are America. Our guitars, our tongues are aimed at you

loaded and heavy as fruit, ready to explode.

## Yes, In 1952 White Teachers Made Their Students Stand Up and Tell the Class What Their Fathers Did for a Living

My father's name is José.
The school said Joe. His father
worked for General Motors
which means we are brown
which means no one
will correct themselves
when he says
*my name is José.*
My grandfather

was an owl, all feathers
the color of moon dust.
See how its light speckled him.
Hear how his beak
cracked a bottle cap.
One for la luna.
One for la lucha.
He flapped his wings over iron

cooling it from 2,000 degrees Fahrenheit.
His talons sparkled as unbreakable
diamonds, while he waited for morning

on the twisted mouths of the tulips.
He was dragged
unconscious from the Plant,

the foreman shouting behind him
*if he's alive, he can come back to work.*

I was there when my grandfather ruffled
the ash from his feathers,
reformed the crease in his fedora
and didn't know yet
he'd be replaced by a machine.

# The Marriage of Frida Kahlo and Diego Rivera

There is so much life
in destruction. A kiss
she didn't digest
like the gold
bullet shell of lipstick
oxidizes and turns
to jade. He says

to eat what she kills
and show her teeth,
no harm here.

How much does she
love him? Enough
to spend all morning
devouring him joint
by joint, each snap
of bone delicious
as her bright
hands make quick
work of all six feet of him.

# Citizenship of the Owl at General Motors

The foreman insists
*owls like the heat.* No
need to ruin a white boy,
where the iron melts
men. Spilled, it beads like mercury
and burns through flesh.
Count what the rocket sheds,

a shotblast bursts through the core.
Without sun Michigan sounds like Michoacán
where his eyes didn't need shielding.
An engine block sealed shut
in the beautiful body of a Chevy.
He casts this metal

heart, a continuous
hum of the line
shaking a path through darkness.
It is the pulse of the owl.
He hears it

as he flies home and strikes
a second time,
on the first song
bird of morning.

# Why I Don't Go to Church

The priest     talks of gardens
but doesn't grow fruit.
Oh, the mess song

birds make. Someday

they will go to seed,
sprout,     and shoot.

A white lab mouse
released into the woods
doesn't have the sense to run.
     Instinct
bred out,

it slips,     head first
like the priest into     collar and gold

embroidery with almond
nails, my grandmother calls
lazy. The film of incense
     a tiny fire     all of it

preserved prayer

    in the pellet    of the owl.

# The Noiseless Flight of Owl Wings

It wasn't a rumor. It was true. My great grandfather flew beside
    Pancho Villa. There was no gold
unless it was in the teeth. Is it possible for the airiness of dust to be a
    kind of common gold,

heavy on eyelashes, wings, horse hooves, and the stretch of cracked
    leather?
It is the part of the land no one lays claim to. A casualty of walking
    with the folded gold

of a corn tortilla in one hand while the other maps great
    grandfather's noiseless
flight. The thing Pancho Villa told his men to imitate at night and
    keep their gold

teeth masked in the mouth. The only drop of light should come
    from the guns aimed at the sleeping
soldiers. The bandolier's beaming bullets hung from the chest in
    salute and gold.

My great grandfather was shot out of the sky, still alive. The federales
    pulled out his feathers
and kept him conscious for three days before they stopped the wind
    from his throat in the gold

of midday. Where sweat, blood, and the fluid that can no longer be
    called tears turned the dust
into mud. His dead wings hidden with corn husks by my great
    grandmother, a golden

eagle before she disappeared and allowed the moon to reflect off her
    forehead in chorus.
The talons of her husband whose call and response had not been
    preserved in a ring of gold.

She ascends to the heavens to braid the plumage of my great
    grandfather Jacinto into Orion's belt.
When I look up I say, *Rico*, and wait for her wings and his eyes to
    recognize me with a flash of gold.

# And When We Return, We Are Water

I am ashamed
to admit how my fingers
swell. My ring
too tight to wear.

The lake filled
with enough
jeweled pollen
and eyes of fish

who keep a light on
and remind me
to wear my watch.
I tell my husband

too much, I can't
keep a secret.
I am afraid of water
and wind.
My love is
a swallow who
dips a wing between
the slick edge of water
and sky. The left hand

in holy water
instead of the right,
a song
I teach my cousins.
Once, I held them

barely above the water.
Their little claws
scratched when they splashed
and shook. *Don't let go*,
but I do.

# Engine Block (Exploded View)

I.  *Patternmaking*

The owl doesn't talk about the distance between him and Lake
    Michigan,
he tries to remove the coal ash from his ear tufts.

2.  *Coremaking*

They rotate. As one owl is dragged out, another is brought in.
Do you think owls are afraid of water?

3.  *Molding*

The owl thinks he hears Lake Michigan when he pours the melted
    metal in the core.
Lake Michigan is iron gray; where is the sun in all this steel?

4.  *Melting and Pouring*

His feathers, sticky corn silk. Did the shakeout make a vibration, a
    wave burning sand?
The foreman doesn't stop counting.

5. *Cleaning*

Not even the owl can see in the dark. A rogue wave buries a freighter.
After twelve hours he forgets light, he forgets water.

# Great Horned Owl

*Tecolote ricinus*


I. *Family*


It must be the ropes, I don't want to make
too much of this—how a vulture
is pulled from a tree
and hung before he can
ever wake up.


II. *Description*


When I say iron
I am talking about the color
gray—as in feathers
close to the skin—
what it means to have
an owl so wet
he cannot fly.


III. *Range*


Brought from México to replace
the bald eagle in Gary, Indiana.

Next to fire—the only light—
waiting for pupils to expand
or collapse, but it was the sound of the train
non-stop, can't be stopped
even for blood on the serrated edges
of feathers.

IV. *Feeding Behavior*

Emerge from the night in
another night. There are women
and a bounty on his head. One dozen
eggs and never enough chiles. The last thing
he put in his mouth
was the heart of a robin, so tiny
she wouldn't miss it.

V. *Nesting and Breeding*

The fragrance is sun and grit. Gunpowder
and all burn. A father, two clutches,
no explanation.

VI. *Songs and Calls*

Against window, open like an envelope,
a small burst of birds, and the territory
of a night sky. This is how
he holds—close hilt. Steel
in the moon, hungry, and his wings
barely touch home.

# Patrilineal

Owls    walk
        before        they can fly.
           My father
    hated    the cold    after
being born in it.
          Too close

     to the train tracks
the sound      is awful
            like the owl
     outside    his window
        and the noise of cats
           thrown        from rooftops.
    I tried to stay under the walnut tree
        but the toast and rank of comino
          brought me back home
    where my father      taught me
the meaning of      hunger.
    The job required

tightened     talons
    around red-hot cylinder heads
    one after another    on the shaker
in the basement of the foundry

where the fire    latched onto clothes    licked
nostrils          in a mist of black dust.        Sea coal
caked    eyelashes        and still

this is how life begins:
a set of        leather gloves        and apron
eight hours of breath        under mask        singed with soot.

When my father clipped        and cleaned    my nails
he        cut them        so
short        they bled.

# Behind the Back of the Robin

Even in the city
the cicadas are heavy
with song and I am
too young to call

a bird anything but red.
What do I
name this, when
the sun enters

my head. I'm afraid
the flowers are blooming again.

When my grandmother feeds
my father I know
to sit still. A girl

at my school eats
ants. She snaps
off their heads and says
*they taste like candy*

and it doesn't scare me
like my grandmother does.

I can't look at her

or the doll she sewed
me, without arms.

When she leaves the kitchen
my father lets me eat.

The sting of menudo sharp,
listening for the sound of her
to return, like a curse.

# Poem in Consideration of My Death

I will die on Sunday afternoon in Saginaw
following a plate of my mother's
enchiladas, fried chicken, and rice.
I will scrape up the congealed queso fresco
and sauce with a tortilla chip, with my
index finger among the garnish of iceberg
lettuce and chopped tomato.
Full, I pour a cup of coffee.
My father is there in his 1986 blue Buick Regal.
If there is a heaven this is it—
the car lot on State Street, my father's smile
as we discuss the different shades of red: candy, burgundy,
cherry, and something that sparkles in-between.
I know I am dead as we drive to pick up tortillas,
the last stop every Sunday.
The day will slice itself into a lemon,
splay its fingers and clean the salt
from its nails as we roll our tortillas
on Grandma Rico's porch made of red tulips.
We cannot eat in the car.
The sun setting is a gold tooth, beyond the
abandoned parking lot covered in dandelions.

The salt and sour of the lemon my final taste of this planet.

My mother will gather her blue robe,

line it with roses, cut like stars.

# The Eagle, Not the United States

Brown wings, like the two hands of my father
holding the tree from falling into Lake Michigan.
The white head of the eagle sees me before I stomp
into the snow, careful for the ice a neighbor
said is there but can't be seen. The reaction
of my foot is the release of the eagle, whose wings
search the wind, spread and part like arteries.
A wave stretches and retreats
across the shore and the eagle notices
the peculiar ripple of a fish. Gone, a rock
worn into the shape of an egg, a fist, heavy
as I imagine the weight of an eagle on my gauntlet.
This isn't the first time I've been left alone, unidentifiable
under a winter coat and hat. I know I am supposed to
lift my hand to everyone and smile, but I stop
when I see an American flag. I walk, pray
for invisibility or like the eagle I curl my feathers
along the bark, stuffing my head underneath
the arc of my wing until this disruption passes.
I go back to water, to the imminent need
for beauty. I am part of this landscape.

# In the Presence of the Robin

Her throne     is     plywood and nails

too many shoes     and house coat

    cover her face


    like the mantilla of the Spanish

doll     as decorative

    as it doesn't belong.


The lace

    of her skirt     a stiff pink,


    smells like radish

and the sticky decay

    of carpet.

If I can invent

    a god, I want the head

    of a vulture.

Beneath each feather,

    a knife.     I heard what they said

    about Mexicans,

    when it rains

leaf and blossom


    sprout from our cars.

The metal unchanged          and bright like a tooth.

        The taste of how          I got here

            is magic                    only to me

   like the bowl of buttered

            brussels sprouts          my grandmother

            kept on her table.

Spoonfuls of the green

   crowns she once wore.

# Set Free

My father        knew doves
were a clenched fist
        under veil.
My mother kept their bodies
like two rings,
        the birds quiet.

My favorite song
        was skittish.    A goodnight
instead of star. The universe

        pecked red      and my father
            set them free.

When I found their wings
        like a jaw
a smudge of black        sunrise
        feathers gone    and the thick

stick of blood    missing from
        their devoted bodies.

# In the One Photo I Have of My Grandmother

The yellow jacket
suspended like laundry

sheets billowing wings
held by a string of a spine

wooden pins charcoaled
wearing away from their metal

coils. A dull abdomen

as in too much sun.
Squint your eyes.

One leg raised to the wind
threatening to take

everything away

in one breath
a word like your name

means both
cold and white

sheets frozen
and shook into

ruled edges

the fragrance
a curled petal

and afternoon.
Your hand

compresses waves
from the tiniest ocean.

## Tomato & Lettuce

Then, everything was garnish,
two kids and a house,
a wife who kept the

beds made, shirts ironed,
secrets hidden like dust

on the canned goods.
What can't be washed
with vinegar—

scum of the coffee pot
or set out in the sun with
fresh linen

my mother swears
had to be ironed
and I believe men

made work for women,
invented tile,

starch, matrimony,
and ama de casa

to chop the tomato

and lettuce sometimes
in bowls, often on the side
as adornment. What
is the relationship

between mother and
daughter, tree and limb,

the moment I say my
memory is not of her
sadness but of her laughter

I've gotten it all wrong
the bright split of my
birth was to a woman

who wanted me
to wear my decoration
a tree cleaned of its bark

after a cool winter doesn't
forget its leaves.

# Mexican in Michigan

Because I know the inauguration is happening and the first woman of color is being sworn into the office of Vice President of the United States, I decide to do something I have never done, and go for a walk alone in the somewhat isolated country of Northern Michigan. The temperature has dropped ten degrees in the last week; it is cold, and I cannot tell if I am listening to the wind or Lake Michigan. Sometimes I am not sure there is a difference. The ground is ninety percent ice, I have a walking stick and crampons, but I move too quickly. I can feel my pulse rise to my face, even though I know there is almost no one in this area, less than ten families for miles. Once I am blocked by a dune, there is a hush of wind, and I hear an almost groan. When I pause to look around, it is the tree bending ever so slightly. I continue, and notice I am walking next to my own frozen footsteps from two days ago. I turn around and put my foot into them to be certain, then continue on to Church Beach.

Walking somewhere always feels longer than it is. I notice the footprints of a rabbit and a crow. I am thinking of my parents and even after fifty-four years of marriage, my father still chokes up about his honeymoon. Not because he loves my mother too much, though he does, but because on the second day Up North my father was hit by a drunk driver. A man so intoxicated that after he hit my father, he kept going at full speed into a telephone pole. When the cops came, they told my father to *calm down*. His 1964 GTO convertible had been destroyed, but it wasn't that. Instead, the cop was giving my father a ticket and demanding he pay for the telephone pole.

I can see the bright white church and Lake Michigan is speaking again. I never get sick of smelling the water before I see it, like the second before it rains. When I clear the dune, I get blasted with the wind from the Lake, and the sun surfaces its head. My face is beginning to burn, but I am smiling. I've lived too long not to do this, to have this moment, these waves, and sea foam dance for me. I wish my parents were with me. I wish this view of brown, to green, to blue, to black was theirs. I try to take a video, but I don't want to look at the screen. Lake Michigan is saying something, she is throwing the veils of her dress, back and forth. She is so loud, I cannot hear the seagull, but watch its shadow. I pull the collar of my wool sweater, that I used as a scarf earlier, back up around my face, and the condensation of my breath has frozen in the time I've been here. I am glad to end the last four years here, on the land of the Odawa, although I don't know what to feel about the church and its garden of crosses. I hold the guard rail; the Lake is an orchestra I thank, the rabbit, crow—and now the arc of my own footsteps—create little disruption.

# John James Audubon and the Battle of San Jacinto

There I was—
on the shelf,
hair suspended
and smooth as
seaweed, the matching
jewel of each
eye and earlobe stretched
soft toward the chin,
a decoration of adornment
never recaptured. Lost,
captioned as missing.
My hands, plucked

like zucchini blossoms
and forever hidden from my head
afloat in formaldehyde—
a specimen labeled
Mexican female.
Glass jar beside
what books, the preserved
body of a burrowing owl
poised toward me, a sash
pistol stolen from Santa Anna after
he dipped his pen betwixt slain soldiers.

A rifle ball

from the occiput

polished bright

as a mirror,

an engagement

ring among the carefully

collected cicatrized skulls, fondled

for a century for indentations and bumps darkly numbered,

classified, confirmation of whose civilization.

# Get Out of the Water

My uncle       keeps
     his birth certificate    in his trunk
          so when
he gets       pulled over   he can prove he was born    in the
  United States.

He calls my father to say *they want us dead.*
     *Who?*                 *All of them.*

My uncle      won't wear a mask
    it happened on what day     of what month
       he stretched   his hand in the dark of the movie
 theater and dipped
     into my father's popcorn.      He ate it all without asking.

My father wants     a picture     of what I look like,
bandana around my face.    Before I go to the grocery
    he says     *when your uncle went back to the store,*
      *the white woman next to him*
        *said she didn't have to wear a mask*
        *and they let her in just like that.*

I've had a headache since

the pines turned yellow       and can't stop

       thinking about       how frightened I was


when my mother took me to see *Jaws*.


*It isn't scary,*       my sister said

       *if you stay*       *out of the water.*

       But they don't,       not until a little white

  boy dies.

       Then, his people       begin to believe

    their vacation might be       ruined or more accurately

they did not    recognize their beach.

       The horror of *Jaws*

is not the rows of teeth,       but the endless sea

       of white faces       who are afraid

       of losing money       knowing the ocean

       has always been full of sharks, blood, and

  everything else they cannot see.

My uncle    can't picture       Adam and Eve

    were ever       naked. He got angry    with me

       as he always does       and told me

       I didn't know what I was       talking about.

Were they    in bathing suits,       standing at the edge of the

  water

*go in,*

*no you go in,*

*I'll go in if you go in.*

What shark        eagerly awaits        to breach

or keeps        swimming and thinks

*I know all about you.*


At the grocery,

my bandana falls        down when I pull the carts apart.

I can hear my uncle laugh,        his too many teeth.

Hands in        my father's

popcorn        and across        his sleeping face.

Next to me,

a man has six bags        of potato chips, a twelve pack

of beer,        and eight steaks.

I can't find        a chicken. I can't remember

what to buy.

Shark attacks often        happen in shallow water.

I've always been        the dog

the owner calls for        and doesn't notice

the stick

floating, not even

the electromagnetic        field

surges a muddy outline

of what I

        know.            Rupture       the stomach
      and find the same license plate,
              milk carton,    and arm       of the
city still wearing its watch.

# Past the Forty-Fifth Parallel

For two days, we are north,
     alone, wanting snow.
          The difference is we are
     afraid, an octave
lower in this gray.
          We haven't     a pear,
     a bartlett won't ruin
the houses where I've seen
          music for two days.
     Say it    saddens us,
          implies we are not
               keeping winter. There were
     ravens, and three     red-bellied
     woodpeckers. Not
in the morning, performing
          twice exactly as assigned.
Lake Michigan
     is a back yard.
          Get the snow, refill
the black and white feathers
          in the woods marked
private     property and never
          step on to     the wrong
               quiet. We don't know because

　　　　morning, afternoon, and evening
look exactly　　　the same.
　　　　The leaf,　　　we keep trying to identify
　　　　as some new bird.

# México City in the Middle of Michigan

A discarded rack
in the woods
a poacher left
his crown damp
with brown moss
behind. No skull.
The leather of his
body gone. His hoof
stomp, a rapid
clap of hands and drag
displace the earth.
The flat sound of the heel
kicked. Count all the points.
The flesh a shrine of braided
muscle and tendons. Chest tuft
a pyramid of breastbone
to a point. Stiff shoulders
pierce each limb forward.
Head poised, pulling the
coarse covering of the skeleton
into bramble and the soft
tug of young bark. The head, once
a twitch too intent for every
leaf snapped. The staccato of his

limbs balancing the chandelier above.
A grand jeté, white belly exposed
like the lifting of a skirt.
Even in nature the men
are seen first. The danger
in desire, a warning,
and sudden dig.
One lick of water.

# Ferment

First, imagine your grandmother
who loved bread telling you not
to get caught up in the exactness

of the recipe which will go
against what the chef taught you
when you were trying to measure

.3 grams, a sixteenth of a teaspoon,
and you thought this is a pinch
as you lifted and replaced each

weight on the scale. Behind you
the dough smelled ripe like beer
in those early mornings of baking school

the machines getting lost
in fold after fold, the ribbon arm of dough
flexible as a twist tie. It is the repetitive motion
that keeps you alive—sardines, a glass of champagne,

falling asleep at 3 PM after work in your whites
forgetting to dot the galaxy of raspberry spit
in Morse code across your sleeves. The boule

round, pulled taught, flexed like flesh and muscle—
holy and alive with breath or excess
expanding like the universe but in your hands

an illusion of control. It's ok not to time
the kneading. Best to do it until you begin to
tire because the dough responds to this

it likes the gentle heat of your hands
the pull, tuck, and snap of applause—
years gone by and yet here you are

somehow, flour on the counter, flour on the floor,
small scabs of dough mark your palms and you
are both elastic and everything.

# The Vows of Frida Kahlo and Diego Rivera

I. *The Dove*

A carnation can't be killed
dirt and work become a flower
I will not eat the faucet's strange spoil
outstretched like a petal
let it flap and fold before dinner.

II. *The Elephant*

What I want to do is punch him
in the mouth, his floppy fish mouth,
and wrap the flesh of his tongue in a tortilla.
I can truss a chicken or a husband.

III. *Notary*

Stitched heart and his neck
spread like the sharp
scales of a fish. The third
eye of the little thief
is a ring, a suture of sunlight
with too much sweet scent.
She thought he was made of hands

because when the lightning split
a tree, it left two masks.
One the monkey stole and the other
burned upright in the fire.

# Resurrection of Prey

How the owl        drags
her body slack and she offers    her head.
        What he splits        with his bill
are soft petals.

        Her ear's soft petal,
conscious        of the snap.
        Don't worry,
                the counter    is clean.
        Her neck,


wrapped and placed    back in her body.


                Head missing,
the heart        and liver        beside a candle
  not death, but        a blessing.


When she counts        to five, he will
        fold his napkin.
Bone, silver,
                and hair.        She is an earring
        and molar.        One pendant of
                our Lady of Guadalupe.


A little water        and the plucked

heads of geraniums            wash her thighs,

    she will save the trusses


blanched in her sweat

    and leave sticky prints on his table.

        He    doesn't like to be reminded of her,

this early in the morning.


There is nothing    he can't catch

and undress.    Catch and undo,    his silent flight.

# Ornithology

To find the owl I must follow the crow
who says my ears and eyes better behave;
it's hard for me to learn what the crow knows

unable to refuse the blueish glow
nor the shiny trinkets my wingtips save.
To find an owl I must follow the crow

who says, into an owl I cannot grow
and takes me to the bend of my eye's grave;
it's hard for me to learn what the crow knows.

The voice of a crow isn't caw but snow,
an arc of ink across a feathered wave.
To find an owl I must follow the crow

pick of pine needles where I was below
pinion of gloss and ash I glide engrave.
It's hard for me to learn what the crow knows.

Lost call of the owl is clouded and slow
wing of midnight and cold blessing me brave.
I keep walking until sun wake and let go;
it's hard for me to learn what the crow knows.

# The Owls of Saginaw

When my grandfather caught
    the long hair of women
        preened in the attic
        of his wings

        with a layer of Vaseline under
    their lipstick kisses
a line of dewy
    red tulips,
        the only
    evidence
    of his hunt.
                *One, two, three.*

He knew his
sons recognized
how cold
    the moon was,
silk against skin. He has always

fed himself

never saying a word
about all those

yellow eyes, flashlights
who mimic him
and believe in prey
by sight.

# Luxury

I know I am not supposed to like it,
alone at the table, peeling the chicken
skin off, and into my mouth. The crisp
salt, sting of hot sauce
stuck to fingers, and I am eating
the prettiest piece first. I served no one
and ate entirely with my hands.
The puff and split of rice browned
in oil with onion and garlic. The sloppiness
of a hand-crushed tomato, a jigsaw
of sweet and acidic. The perfume of cilantro,
no doubt stuck in my teeth and flesh of chicken
spurred to greatness with a rub of comino.
The tortilla torn apart, breathing
because its perfect edge was singed by fire.
The rinse and spin of digestion, a splash more
wine to soften when I think I am
a dandelion blown apart
curved like the bill of a hummingbird
and thigh. My heart is never still,
bloomed, outstretched, and
foolish. When I squeeze a cut
lemon, I close my eyes. Robins
can't be captive, they die

within moments of human contact.

I'd rather let them fly

next to the orange butterflies, and

shake the dull sepia feathers

located on the belly, which are slightly

brighter on men.

# Elegy for My Quinceañera

Over my mother's dead body, I arrive
dressed in the traje de charro,
my father's Gibson Les Paul strapped to my chest
with one red carnation behind my ear.

Dressed in the traje de charro
singing *Paloma Negra* bringing my tías to tears
with one red carnation behind my ear.
My necklace of Guadalupe blessed by my grandmother

singing *Paloma Negra* bringing my tías to tears.
The tamales slip out of their dresses.
My necklace of Guadalupe blessed by my grandmother
resplendent in marigolds. On a tablecloth of jeweled green

the tamales slip out of their dresses
when we talk too loud, not because of the music
resplendent in marigolds, on a tablecloth of jeweled green.
I will stain my lips with hibiscus

when we talk too loud, not because of the music.
My father's Gibson Les Paul strapped to my chest,
I will stain my lips with hibiscus
over my mother's dead body, I arrive.

# Each is Another and No Other

And there it was,
the aftermath of my
dinner. The orange lick

around the burner, bright
spheres of fat suspended before
they stain. I will not

find the spot until morning
under the chest,
quick and eternal.

Being a good cook means
cleaning up and having an
oven that won't heat properly

much in the way as being in love
means hurt, the sudden cut
of fingernail and then into finger

nothing I've made tastes
like a picture.
The knife a decoration

and I hated my husband
when he bought me
a cookbook

everyone said
I was so lucky
cooking was *easy*

the kitchen was
where women went to die
not to be born as dishwashers

day drunk, the pain in my feet
holy, and in my apron is the face
of water. You pick the sink:

wash, rinse, or sanitize.
One will say more about you
than me. The steam comes off my hand

for minutes, caught in sunlight.
Why must everyplace have too many windows
and girls who won't pull back their hair?

The curled edge of a blade seems
easy to hone like the stick of garlic,
and the taste of a little blood.

I was never a very good
daughter, I let my mother
do everything and thought her a fool

who drew smiley faces
with mustard on every
single bologna sandwich.

# Learning to Sail, I Can Only Think of Odysseus and Ask to Be Tied to the Mast

What did Odysseus do besides sleep with spiders?

There was no such sixth finger on Anne Boleyn.

I slowly repeat bowline and make a small loop.

Odysseus ate charred meat, the heart

of his wife peeled apart in sections like fruit.

I am made of spiders.

I pull them from my hair each morning.

I let them go, watch the wind

shift toward a wing and terrify

my spine into a bird.

The boat is a delicious

insect blown over the lake, ignorant

of the swallow.

Wind swells around me, takes its

tongue and presses me to the roof of its mouth.

I float above what has turned into marriage.

The fragile film of what you thought

I was and what I

thought I would become.

Yes, dear—

I haven't eaten

all your ribs

dipped in sauce and kept

warm with a piece of white bread.


There is something stuck

on my bicuspid.

Seagulls blanket the lake, drift on the wake after

I reach again to touch.

Close enough to stretch my welted

wrist as a jewel.

Nothing is still, even this water

trembles with flies.

The bruises on my knee

        raise, a full glass to my mouth.

To fail and keep going

    makes me feel ridiculous, as I

        watch the egret fly.

On my knees to the wind

      waiting for its fingers

  to wrench the sails loose.

No one but Odysseus

  notices that I am

    a series of small movements

      on the edge of want

  without sirens

    without women, only men.

The ducks delay

  arrival, waiting

  for the men to put on a shirt and shut

their mouths.

I try to sleep

    alone, covered

        with the stink of

            Odysseus and a flashlight

                of the moon.

      I keep my back to the wind.

        There is no, I remember

      to move forward.

I place a star on my

        right foot, star foot.

       If I fall, I will wait to swim

       and let the cool

           mouth of the lake

         drink my spine.

   Oh Odysseus, the dead

          are with me

                                    because I

                        remember them.

            There is no apology

                    for hunger and conquest,

                    each leaves his name.

# Robin

*Purépecha guadalupana*

I. *Family*

Slick fish stunned
and head thwacked.
The eyes, a magnet
with scales like laces.
One ripe avocado.

II. *Description*

A bird, mostly belly
toothpicks for legs
always the dull feathers
of the females.
Look closely

the cluster of white
glacier on the eye
stings fingertips
long after they've removed
seeds from a chile.

III. *Songs and Calls*

With or without a sister
but not without light.
One small shift
and the strike of her
splits the skin.

IV. *Range*

Michoacán misplaced in Michigan.
A grito dazzles midair
spins its skirt. Hem loose,
the string an almost forest.

V. *Nesting and Breeding*

Speckled jewel on the train north
hidden like a bad
tooth in the fan of a smile.
Turquoise not blue.
The black ink of a love letter
scratching against the sky.
She will build and will

vanish lineage of who
looks like who.

VI. *Feeding Behavior*

The ground, a full mouth
after rain. A pulse of her
bends daylight and stomps
and stomps. Sharpening
her nails on every stone.

# Shotblast

*en memoria de mi tío*

Dear Saginaw,

    build me a car

        metal gray, gun

            and the body of my uncle

                who couldn't be saved in his brown

                    skin. In my dream he is silent,

                gray snow silent

                    in the tires of Saginaw.

     Camouflage brown

        rust on the car

            door which is open, and uncle

            with no gun.

The first gun

    was given, was silent

        from my father to my uncle.

            You have the serial numbers, Saginaw.

            A bullet bright, car

                spark caught in the brown

                muscle of earth. Brown

              like a gun

                handle rolls the car

                         windows into silence
                         crossing the Saginaw
                         River to identify my uncle

the body of my uncle
        seeped in the brown
                 edge of pine in Saginaw.
                     The shotgun
            blast across his chest silencing
                 the metal car

                    frame of his body, the careful car
                      door open above my uncle
                        outstretched, those wings silent
                      when they close back into the brown
                           leather hand and grip of a gun.
        The shock and Saginaw

collapse into the gravity of bridge and uncle. Brown,
remarkably so, the beautiful structure of silence and birds
     with their gun
beaks tapping out one car engine at a time. Did you hear
     them, Saginaw?

# The Universe, According to Rufino Tamayo


Past the breath         stars have
      I find myself    an open hand of night


pupils eclipse the moon.
      The blackness underneath my feet,    not above
        where the    sky is filled with sea.
      My eyelash shields    the arm    of the galaxy
        with one word,
             *here.* I shake
               my hair like a cloud
          and let the spirals of my curls dot
            the hereafter    with quasars.
I have no need to crush    darkness,
        only hold    my hand out to it
          like the five    fingers of my lungs


            expand and collapse.
I have hidden    my teeth    for days. I'm afraid they
            will spill and become
      silver streetlights    in competition with the marble
              gleam of the moon.
    My sharp points are a reminder    I am atmosphere.
The snap of my fingers makes stars pulse,
        smashed lilacs of my eyelids crumble

into the depths of the ocean under moonlight
and the whisper of the most delicate dove.

I fear I will never eat.   I fear my tongue
                            will hang itself on an ice cube.
Marigolds in front of me like pursed lips,
                      arms spread      as an echo.

I may disappear,        but if I spell my name
            I return like dusk      and pray to never fall asleep.

# Ode to the Grocery

The folds of the     carnation differ from     the dog ear     of the rose,
the sticky     paper of baby's     breath, or the closed     mouth of the tulip
turning     toward the fur     of the sunflower head; the way     glads are
always soaking          wet and look like they've          been hacked,
prehistoric—like curling     ribbon     between     thumb     and     scissor     in
one zip     or it rips like     the shark     skin of an orange          and its
puckered     belly button;          the regularly     priced rotten avocado
caving in     my hand, shaking     water from     radish leaves,     and the
polished     cheek of a     tomato     separated from its     pungent     stem.
I miss     knocking     on a watermelon     and asking *is anybody home;* my
father rolling     a cayenne     between his     fingers     and counting the
pop     of each     seed; bright     lemons and     limes     pressed     under the
weight     of my     palm into a wheel     of fainting pulp;     the noble
shallot,     hidden     behind     the garlic, dirty     and forgotten untamed
cousin to the     onion; mushrooms     still clinging     to earth, concealing
their circle     of gills     from the     parsley     who will demand     they be
removed, so as     to     not     cloud the sauce;     the shawls     of lettuce,
ruffled     collars, and     pleats     so     perfect     they should be displayed in
their entirety—     uncut and     spun;     the weight of an asian pear     in my
hand,     each bite     a spill     and suck     that cannot     stop the escaping water.

# Second Shift

A thunder through the chest.

All metal and two hundred pigeons
cannot cover the fire
from rafter to machine.

The heat crawls under
hard hat

a slap of summer
so heavy

it is an engine.

The carbon in nodular iron
rings like crystal

along my father's collar.

He pretends his sleeves are waves,
not the stiff denim
my mother irons, buttons,

and hangs. The delicate stitch
of my father's hand removed

the white thread along the edge
of a pocket to make room
for his mechanical pencil.
I don't know

if I will inherit

his shirt. After repeated
washing, it fades into a phantom

blue, like the eyes of my husband

whose shirts have never been
stretched out like a wing

held and seared with metal.

# Hooked Lace

I was always in the good car with my mother, the one
unable to be kept at the plant because of knives

in tires and cigarettes left lit on paint.
She hated the Z-28. She wanted four doors, not two,

after a hard rain she hit every puddle and pothole.
Each splash, pasted and caked, left to dry

overnight like a sin. My mother collected Queen
Anne's Lace, tall crowns masquerading as weeds

the cluster of petals small as a flea
like gnats accidentally inhaled—

a universe to another creature. Birds are not
safe until they fledge and learn

to distinguish between hemlock and carrot. Simple
as a seed taken for seven days to stop an egg from embedding.

# Hand Over Heart

I didn't laugh when     a woman       said      all
Mexicans carry knives. I felt for
         mine      in my pocket,         it's justice
         defined by      how often I use it      and
never in a fight,       but the liberty
      to open or fix any thing with
         one swipe—a routine     like my father     indivisible
      from his car,     driving    to work every    day, like a god
whose    power    is to assemble     an entire vehicle     in under
      or exactly       sixty     seconds        with a nation
      of machines      mastered       like the control of one
          tool      stamping       metal and stands
              the frame upright—it
            self a shell of edges     which
        spark and ride     a belt for
           my body,        a republic
       assembled by nails         and hooks, the
          abdomen of dragonflies     to
        beat my heart, and
        with this     I can hear America
           as a song     I can't turn off of
the Saginaw River      left     in states
       so toxic     a legacy     of factories united
       parasitically through the

middle of

            my city      like a flag

        folds    before it falls.    The

East and West    still separated   by a bridge    that doesn't rotate to

    keep who away from whom    as an allegiance

    the walleye, the peony as my pledge

    to not begin and end with I.

# Brain Food

At night
we removed
their bodies
from under
the sticky
plastic wrap,
dug our fingers
inside their bellies
and tugged their flesh
toward our mouths.
The sparkling
gold eyes,
back bones,
and sleek shells
on the table
smelling of smoke
and iron.
*Brain food*,
my father said
and tapped
my head.

# Hemingway Country

When did departure make me
nervous to drink water, and instead
focus on a piece of gum

tiny particles of mint hidden in
the glacial recesses of my molars.
The first time

I was pulled over
the cop asked what I was doing
going 30 in a 25.
Answering felt hardly worth it.
I am sick of white people

and their cottages,
so what if they don't lock their doors.
When I went crazy
I couldn't eat

the banana bread my mother gave me.
If I put it near my mouth,
the thought of not having any more
became too great

like the game I played as a child

naming every object in my room
before falling asleep as *the last*,

until I got to myself.
My cousin said I was never very good at math

even the three hours it takes to get up north
are an eternity.
I haven't stopped at a public restroom in years.

My father says if we lived in a different state,
he could've never married my mother.
He shouts towards her,
he would've been arrested and thrown in jail.
Not long ago,

my father let me hold
a pistol with both hands and said
*below the waist isn't a felony*.
My husband stood before me
and we weren't married then,
he hadn't taken me to Petoskey

nor had I seen him glide along the water

as his favorite bird:

half airplane

and half boat.

I wanted him to think I could

shoot him and not myself

as if violence made it possible

to understand love.

I didn't like sleeping

in the woods, although

I only tried it once.

Everything shut

up when I realized

I could be in love

unabashedly

soaking and

savoring the

body of Lake Michigan.

A small prayer of an afterlife

among the mayflies
who return as water.
The curved crest

in the eyes of my husband
blue as heron and gray
as a hull caught in the wing
span of a wave tempering
the edge of my plate.

# Lessons on Becoming Full Grown

Young, my father painted my room pink & I thought
this is what little girls do. I screamed
when my brother said he would cut my hair.

I didn't mind dresses when jeans were too hot & green
was my grandmother's favorite color.

She was mean. I told everyone I knew

football players practiced ballet. I read
a ballerina lived off a piece of cheese & six ounces of milk.

This hardly means a thing now,
my room white & decorated in shadows. A half dead
crabapple. I haven't danced

in years. My instructor drank herself to death.

She came to class in casts & covered in bruises.
I thought it was from dancing. I thought she practiced so hard she
    fell. I can still smell

the leotards & tights, sweet with sweat. How they laid on the body
    then & didn't pinch.
How the older girls

told me my boyfriend would be *lucky*. Tap shoes with a heel in silver.
It ended so quickly. My mother tying up my hair & filling in my lips
    with red.
She tried hard to tame it, wrapped it in plastic bags with hot oil.

I wrapped my Barbie in electrical tape. There are pictures. I cut my
    own hair

& I know, it looks better long. Who am I kidding?

When I married, I didn't want to believe
this was the best I would ever look. My mother
took off my glasses & told me I was pretty.

Metal dug into my chest & I stepped on my own ridiculous hem.
My armpits red from the chafe of lace & *I can't believe you
wore white*. Once,

I dressed as a white girl. Spent $20 on the costume:
plaid skirt, sweater vest, with my own patent leather Mary Janes.

I straightened my hair. My boyfriend

kept smoothing my head with his hand. Next to me,
a guy pulled his fingers apart & stuck his tongue between them.

My boyfriend said it was like kissing someone else.

It was supposed to be a joke

like when my father couldn't get my brother to shave. He took out
the razor's blade & let me froth the Barbasol on my face.

Slowly, I went across the delicate stretch of skin beneath my chin
& up to a swath of cheek. *Look, look how easy this is.*

I saved my upper lip for last
& curled it taut over my teeth, angling my face. Oh

how I wanted to do this every Sunday before we washed the car, before

my father closed my hand & said *like this, otherwise you'll hurt
yourself when you punch somebody.*

# What I Found

Lilac sheets      frayed on one edge

           the course hair of my father's

                     neck more

                     furniture than space

an alarm clock       my uncle    made orange

                     silk pajamas

                     a pretty dress

                     never my mother

                     answering above

                     cash    in an envelope

                     another drawer

                           a slip of paper

          grocery list:

          daughter

          name _____

          date of birth

Hallmark cards
diary of temperatures
glasses never worn
seeds of morning
glories my father
planted along the fence

I ask my cousin what sex is

    & blush        afraid to kiss
        any boy
            how interesting
                shave the leg    nick the knee
witness the length      drawer open
        slip of paper in hand
          daughter    with a name
              not mine    what two people can do

# Feeding Rituals

Robins, unlike my grandmother,
return to México.
Instead, she divides

flour, egg wash,
and cornmeal into bowls.

Lemon cut
and Bless us

O Lord and these Thy gifts.
There is no way I will
pray to a man

or let him eat first.
A catfish can live

outside of water for hours.
She tugs the flesh free
and feasts completely
by herself; its body
a twitch of nerves.
Afternoon
is a flash

underneath the black
of her comal.

I won't dare
open my hand,
another gaping mouth.

# Sacrament

I want to say twelve, although I hope it was earlier when
I came home and found my mother asleep

my mother asleep under her single-stitched
afghan, it took her three years to make.

It took her years to learn how to make tamales, because my
grandmother was secretive and wouldn't wait

she wouldn't wait for my mother to show up,
she'd finish the tamales by noon and brew a pot of coffee.

Always with a cup of coffee, because tamales are too rich.
Often my mother had to guess what was in what,

what was in the tamales was manteca, swaths of it,
so much lard, my mother didn't believe it

she didn't believe I would want to help her. Not with the
meat, it was too fatty. Not with the chiles, they were too hot.

The chiles were so hot, we wore gloves to remove
the stems and seeds. Gloves to peel back the fat

like peeling back the corn husk slowly to check the masa. Another
    coffee cup of water
poured anywhere inside the pan. The towel to tuck them in stained
    red, everything

stained red. T-shirt, hands, my jeans, the kitchen table,
forks, knives, and even the masa hardened on the floor was red.

Hardened on the floor were shreds of meat, husk hair,
pork grease, and crumbs of the cookie I ate

the cookie, a little pig from the bakery
where we ordered fifteen pounds of masa.

Fifteen pounds of masa I beat and coaxed with my
hands, bright red every Christmas, a gift for my family.

A gift for my family: uncle, cousins, tías one and two,
a rite to my mother, the tamale pot stuffed into a snowbank to cool,

the pig, chiles, and manteca. A ceremony to her hands,
her hands with the wrinkled knuckles, scarred from psoriasis. Those
    hands,

that wrote down exactly, how many bags of chiles, pounds of pork,
    blocks of manteca,
corn husks, the hours from start to finish. Her hands were the first
    to hold me.

# En Español Por Favor

In México
> my husband hands me
> the menu. This is the same thing
my father
> did to combat my shyness
> when teachers thought I couldn't speak.
Somehow
> I didn't die, as I hoped.
> My face, fire when I remember I
never knew how
> to address my grandmother.
> Oh god
to disappear.
> Everything was green,
> even the edges of her embroidered towels
> when she said
> *I love you*, in English.
Look,
> my mother put me in Spanish classes and my father
> taught me how to change a tire.
My grandmother
> didn't become a U.S. citizen. She kicked a priest
> out of her house for saying she had Spanish blood and

never talked about México.

    I point to my husband, *no come carne.*

# Optics

It's hard for me to look
directly at my sister;

she's so small I think
of all the ways I could

hurt her. She still doesn't
know how to swim. She's afraid

to touch my hair.
I can hardly keep

from shivering. How many
versions of me

will she delete? It's easy
to retell the story

when I was in New York
I thought I saw her leaving

a bus or getting
on another subway

though I should've
said something, I didn't.

*It's ok to smile.*
I want her to tell me

*touch your ear,*
*look to the left,*

or to make
me apologize

for our father choosing
my mother.

Not once have I
kissed my sister.

Whose dream
was it to dress

us in the same outfit?
When I threw mine away

the stitch of a gene pool
all undertow

too much
before and after

in the time it takes
to make my sister
afraid of water forever.

# Shade Tree Mechanic

Air thick
with oil,
dead tires,
and work

the same oil
leaves a halo
from my father's
head, while
he sleeps

oil, under
nails, on the collar
of coveralls that
are dark blue, anything
to hide the oil
even the well
of Lava soap
smells like oil
and so does
the cardboard

my father saves
because cement
is cold on our backs.
I twist

the washer
and let
the still
warm oil
pool in a bucket.

I want to smell
like this metal,
oil, and my father
who this close
to an engine
is gentle when
he wipes the oil
from my hands
which look like
his hands,
amber as new oil.

I have never
been closer to being
a better daughter,
almost a son.

# Where the Girls Are

Above the river the great blue heron
is graffiti reflected in the neon lettering
puddled in pools against the muddy edges
I used to walk, years ago in my father's leather jacket

stiff like the train tracks beside the river, laundry-
lapped sleeves disguising themselves as waves, fifteen
thousand work shirts un-ironed, left for the layering
of a bird's nest in waiting. There are no fish at this shore.

My best friend's mother was a prostitute; I didn't know.
My father told me she asked him once if he
and his friends would like to party with her and her

friends, the ones she worked with at Second National Bank, the
    building
she took me to and let me and her daughter stand in the fourteenth-floor
window, close enough to be a handshake or someone's favorite color.

# In My Own State

Never let go my skin.
Lake Michigan is
the bed I make, a
sandwich, and sea

bird daringly close.
I have covered my
body for too long, even
my scars are

a memory
to time and light.
An almost ocean
truncates the sharp

point of my ankle.
How much piss
fills this shore?
The first time I saw

bottled water I
thought of the olive
jar my mother kept
in her dresser.

I was in L.A.
which felt far
enough to be sacred.
Chlorine could make

a body glow after
days spent in the
public pool. Lake
Michigan was for

someone else, even
the waves clap white.
Will I smell like earth?
Sand and stone. The

glimmer of one fish.
After the first four
months of water, it's
the movement of land

spinning on an axis. I attach
my feet to the legs of a table.
Lake Michigan is an arrhythmia.
One, one thousand. Two.

# What Remains of General Motors

Hollow houses redolent of fire
buckle beside train tracks threaded

through grass
rather than nail.
The shattered cement ruptures
wildflowers,
some might say
weeds, but aren't
they gorgeous
the way they crawl

one stem after another
exposing the gates
jagged like a split
rib cage.

A shock
of lavender home to pigeons
still dusted with coal.
The faceted face of a watch

doesn't say

       thank you. Instead,

it clouds.

## La Patria

Everywhere I hear
my grandmother
call me. I didn't expect
an egret, slick
with white wings
to sink like marble
or to memorize
how Spanish kneads
my tongue into pulp.
I laugh when I forget
the word for ice, touch
a thousand purple trumpets
and look again
for my grandmother
in a butterfly wing.
I'm no good

in big cities, too worried
I'm lost until I
unwrap a tortilla
revealing its heart
of huitlacoche.
The limes slight

as songbird eggs
I clutch

the metal pendant
around my neck. Once
my brother said I looked
like her. He meant mean,

he said *meaty*. My necklace
sets off an alarm at the airport.
I shout *Lupe, Lupe, La Señora*.
The guard lets me go.

# Get Out of My House

Almost morning, she sings with her sister who says she never visits
    enough.
I want her like this, a little drunk, laughing. *Ay*.

My father didn't sleep last night. He pictured her
hidden in the folds of her apron, *come tus chícharos. Ay*.

Two portraits hung in her living room. La Virgen de Guadalupe
and her son. Young, I worshiped them. *Ay*.

It wasn't a joke when she kicked me out of her house.
Gone like the piece of chocolate cake she ate quickly. *Ay*.

I know better now, why she hides her face
from the tree whose branches she broke. *Ay, Mónica*.

# What General Motors Doesn't Protect

I drive in wide circles, the click
of my steering is a card hitting a spoke

my father tilts his head,
all sound

is interruption.
The engine amplified

when played back from a brick wall.

My father worked
in a landscape

of machines lit by spark.
Sheared metal matches

seven days a week.
A meteor shower

too close to earth.
The wooden dowel he presses

against his ear, the other
end to the engine.

In bright sun my father
focuses on the maple,
*tell me when the cicadas start singing.*

# To Skip a Stone

Dear Lake Michigan,
I wasn't always afraid
of you. Not in the traditional
sense, because when my mother
said I ought to be having fun,
I did. It was awfully hard
not to. She pulled me from
your shores to jump waves;
I didn't think we'd die,
she wouldn't let me.
Twice we came to you. My mother

called me a water bug and a lifetime.
Everywhere we went, I shook, asked
her to tell me how she met my father.
The story I memorized. A double
date and my father couldn't keep his
eyes off her fuzzy hair. He called it
*kinky*, making her blush every time.
I am a tourist to you

counting the number
of chirps a cricket makes
to estimate your temperature.

Cold.
I have never seen you

in the winter, where you are
hidden, cavernous, and very
alive. To you I will walk,
listen for the whisper
of a bird wing, the crack
of snow beneath my boot,
one at a time like how I stop
breathing on a boat from
memory, and remind myself

I know how to swim.
My mother is watching
as always, listening for me
to growl as I did when
she left the room.
Tiny animal, she thought,
and let me chew on bones.
All her songs are wrong
and unpredictable like your waves

yet I come back,

the wrong color and expectation.

Beside you as gently as my mother

set me in the canoe. I swear

it was hours, years, we floated,

and I touched you like a fish

in stillness. The stick of you

swollen in every pore and when I

slept your sand leaked from my feet.

No one can consume the sun

in one billowing curtain like you do.

Say goodbye, and let me roost

in the depth of you. Shipwrecked

to the sound of you all light

and wind rise.

# Northern Cardinal

*Cardinalis madrelis*

I. *Family*

I don't know
if I tried talking to god

rather, I thought of my mother,
my grandmother,
and then crossed myself
to pray to them.

II. *Description*

I miss the smell of her,
Coca-Cola on ice and hair spray.
The smear of her red bikini
brought heat lightning.

III. *Range*

This does not change;
the church never cared about
how many dandelions
I took for my mother.

IV. *Feeding Behavior*

It's impossible
for me to separate
when my mother was sad
and the priest who recommended
she re-read the Book of Ruth
and lie beside my father's feet.

V. *Nesting and Breeding*

The day my mother considered
leaving my father, she called to
the voice of god

as birds do—
mimic carefully and
unbraid the cord like pressing
a pearl into her ear

she addresses the cardinal
who responds before I can see him;
sometimes she is a decoration and
everything is song.

VI. *Songs and Calls*

She reminds me I'm just like my father

whose seat I take
after washing the dust off two wine glasses

etched with doves.
I know she's unhappy.

At night, I steal money
from my father's wallet and put it in her purse.

# Soy De La Luna

*For the Two Thousand Three Hundred
Immigrant Children Separated from their Parents*

I can count to two
thousand and three
hundred in two hundred and
thirty minutes.
Let me start with

mi'jo, mi'ja, mi vida, petunia.
My heart beats two thousand and four

hundred times in half an hour.
Mi'jo, mi'ja,
mi vida, petunia.
I'll lose two thousand and three

hundred hairs in twenty-three days.
Mi'jo, mi'ja,

mi vida, petunia.
I'm trespassing once

I stop moving.
Mi'jo, mi'ja

mi vida, petunia.
The breath from my lungs is ninety

percent moon dust.
I can hardly breathe,
mi'jo, mi'ja,
mi vida, petunia.
My heart broke the day my mother

told me I would
outlive her. I cried so hard
I couldn't breathe,
mi'jo, mi'ja,

mi vida, petunia.
I dream of a bridge covered
in lions' heads, their tongues
a full moon.
Mi'jo, mi'ja,

mi vida, petunia.
My blood has turned to wine.
I forget to breathe,

forget to look
for the moon.
Mi'jo, mi'ja,
mi vida, petunia.
The lilacs' bloom

doesn't last.
A girl turns into a fawn

moon blocked by streetlights.
How awful to
hide those white
splotches, bits of

moon dust against
the grass too wet, wept with tears.

Mi'jo, mi'ja,
mi vida, petunia.
I carry the dark

of her eyes, the
recommended amount
of sodium is two

thousand and three
hundred milligrams
every day. Salt is

from the sea.
The sea's tide
is controlled by the
moon which says
mi'jo, mi'ja,
mi vida, petunia.
The Arctic Tern travels to the moon
three times during its life.
I trust them to carry all two
thousand and three
hundred home.

# Domesticate

Dear grandmother,
was it my eyes that gave me away? Green
instead of gold. Who hid the remote?
It's one thirty and your novela is on.

I am not allowed to love you
or all your dresses.
I dream of a little girl who will not speak. I feed her

bread with cinnamon and butter.
Something is wrong in my kitchen. The enchiladas

are hard to make. I am covered in oil, splatter to the ceiling.
Is it too late for hot chocolate? Grandmother,
why do you bring me to your house at night?
Let me
roast you a chicken. I will share the wings,
pull the tender meat from the neck,
and remove the oyster of each thigh.

It's those goddamn jesses I can't stop looking at,
how they hang from under your skirt. Grandmother,
I know this is part of the process.
Fry each tortilla in oil and sauce,

crumble the queso fresco and chop the white onion.
To think I once got sick of this meal.
The way my mother made it—

serving my father first.
You didn't see her like this

scratching her ankles,
the leather straps barely visible.

# Five Things Borrowed

*after Sandra Cisneros*

I wanted to
      and did leave Saginaw.
         My Spanish is

            concealed

because       I ask too much from
           the smell

        of lemons.
I am the woman who

didn't take

her husband's name, or
have children.

      No one        wonders when

        I will grow a vegetable garden
          or if

        I liked New York. I have

not changed my

phone number

in twenty years.
When the daffodils bloom

I bring them inside.
I have yet to see

a person
along the Huron River

lost in bird song

waiting to return

to sky.

I grew up

with the privilege
of     a     father
who looks

exactly         like me

and     I learned     the most
        from dishwashing

when my brother's wife ran off to Jamaica

all he ate

        was grits     for breakfast. Then

                when she came back
                        my mother-in-law wanted to teach me

the correct way

                to wash her son's shirts.

The last time
        I was a ring
                was after a party

everyone home and apron

around my neck. The time I heard the geese

traveling with the moon

I believed I was hallucinating and now when they wake me

I know I'm not and imagine I am

an owl            falling swiftly
on the sound.

# Birds of a Feather

As the crow flies, so did my father
before work, after work, between two
houses like a swan bats his wings
over the water and flies as free as
a hawk, dazed from dipping in thermals.
My mother stayed home, eagle-
eyed, counted cans of tomato sauce
and stripped avocados, dropping
their pregnant bellies like a nest.
My father an early bird eager to do
another swan dive from the links
in my mother's watch, hollow as a
ribcage. Under wing a broken
song like an ugly duckling isn't ugly
but unique, and stands out like the flightless
dodo who trusts because it is too awful not to.

# Forecast

I was never excited
by the clouds
the way they
move fast
pulled across
the vast sky
as if they have
somewhere to go
an appointment,
a bus line, the
circular path of a train.
I remember I haven't
talked to my sister
since Biden was
elected. I told her
I couldn't take,
I didn't have the energy for,
I no longer wanted to,
and needed a break from

her. When the clouds
are tugged through
the sky I know weather
is coming. Thick sheets

of rain and the trees
finally get to sing,
move their arms
in tune
with the crow
who is a high
hat, the blue jay a
cymbal, the weeds
an audience

they too dance
and sway. My sister
has always been some-
where else, half of some-
thing I don't understand,
don't have an answer for,
and when I talk about it
now, I've never
wanted to go

to Mars or the moon
too attached to atmosphere,
the wind putting my hair

into my mouth. I pull
they push. I don't get

sick of this game
the clouds losing
a piece of themselves
in wisps and wing

the way in which
I have never held
my sister's hand
may mean I
cannot love her

or I am afraid
of the coming
rain. The
absence of her
uncomplicated
as the trees
shed themselves
and enter every

piece of me,
a silly
replica of
a house.

# Only the Snow Will Quiet the Robin

I loved her, knowing she
pecked my father ceaselessly.

She had *meat hooks* he said.
Her mirror, empty

as the picture she kept of her sister,
almost a twin.
Let me get this straight,

mating is more violence than pleasure.
I don't know if she loved

my grandfather, who could eat
a dozen eggs for breakfast while
her belly swelled.

When the body of my grandmother fell
like snow, my father and I crawled into
the kitchen cupboards.
There was no owl to stop her.

# Figurehead

I misunderstood.
The first woman sailor I met

had one eye and a husband
who called her *Happy*.

She hated it.

Ears plugged, blood
hums from the shell;
I am hearing myself

recite the names of Mercury
astronauts because women
on boats are bad luck.
I didn't say excuse me to the tiller

I shouldn't be,
the way a fish doesn't care
when he touches me.
My leg, fishnet and hawk—
holding myself
underwater doesn't have the desired effect.
I wait to grow gills and rise. I wouldn't survive

one kiss on each cheek.
Bueno. Bueno. Bring me a bird

as unloveable as a seagull.
My husband doesn't like

when I wear lipstick.
I guess what they say is true,
breakfast before
worm, and hook.

Last night I dreamt
I didn't comb my hair
or let my food digest. I can
forget on my own—
the shadow overhead
and overheard.
I am underwater
before and during
the time it takes
to make a bird
a boat, and call
them both women.

# Analog

I don't dream I'm nature's
dusty sun. Often, I first
look out a window and I'm certain of the green
blanket of land I've tried to sleep on twice. Is
this separation of body and breath what makes gold
shift hands, decorate a rocket, her
exterior a recording—the soundtrack to humanity or at its hardest,
graffiti of a man and a woman. The sketch and hue
of their simple shapes another dark line to attach meaning to,
a set of advantageous languages to hold
or die. Two humans blessedly indistinguishable, except for the eye
   of her
belly, a spiral of cells held in gestation too early
to contend with gravity or the pause of a leaf
suspended, before returning into itself. When is
the complaint of my form more than a
voyage of vice I capture like a ripe flower
on the verge of tumbling toward earth, but
not forever like the swift reel of memory. Only
once is the slip, made easy under so
much rain. A collection of will. An
income measured by legend instead of the hour
I began to coat the walls with every last dove then
the equation for photosynthesis trapped in a leaf.

The quick tug of silence subsides

from articulation of pulse. *Always better to*

*start over than to never start again* said the leaf

near the oblivion of a collapsing red giant, so

depleted of its hydrogen it decided to Eden

itself—a late happy birthday and the candles sank

into the knees of the cake. To

start singing would be ridiculous. A party of grief

could easily crush a hotel of a brain, so

eager to book each guest and kick them out at dawn.

I wouldn't know what to pack. Nothing goes

with gamma rays, each wave a splashdown

in a dream with too much spark to close my eyes to.

I don't like how the planet rotates and shortens the day.

I keep waking up earlier, nothing

but a screech owl to distinguish between night and morning. The

fall of gold

butter in craters of sourdough keeps me alive today, and I can

begin to understand why I want to stay.

# The Robin Who Turned to Snow

Day-moon, open the mouth of a robin.

She knew before I did
       men do whatever the fuck they want

¡Mira!
       but never point at the budding plants

who will wither with the attention.
       The white wings of her rebozo

wouldn't have survived the kitchen
       let us crawl into the cupboards.

The flash and roar of her,
       a shock of snow in August

Dios te salve María
       jagged are the heads of carnations

she's come for the feathers
       of birds who crush their necks

bright with blood
       the first sound of light

is a swallowed pearl

      her claws scratch then steady

when she throws me in the air,

      I pivot toward home.

# My Mother and the Cardinal

According to my mother I make everything up. I don't
know if she likes me when I call her by her first name.

She picks too many strawberries.
I try to eat them all
caked in sugar,

the white bowl blush.
My mother in a sheer blouse
is beautiful, I think

I can't be hers.
She says, *birds can talk,*
*pretty, pretty, pretty, pretty, pretty*.

I can always spot a cardinal,
his red head and black mask.
My mother made her own wings

from an eye pencil, drove her mother mad.

The cardinal loved her,

even when she followed my father to work.
If he hadn't died,

my feathers would be red.

# A Lesson from My Father About Electricity

When I wait
for my father the stars

disappear. Only bats
dart and flutter

hungry for the hum
of mosquitos thick

as honey, whose bright
sting lingers and jumps

like electricity can.
*It's looking for a body.*

He didn't say
how production
stopped when the volt
distribution panel was
cleaned of calf and hip.
No matter how hot

the summer was my father
said it was nothing compared

to coke, spelled *coal*. The way it
penetrated his skin like the breathlessness of asphalt
and the charcoal briquettes he set fire to—

the sizzle and curl of chicken skin
rubbed with paprika, salt, and black pepper.
The acrid spray of vinegar when turned and sealed
under lid. I stood next to the heat,
a sticky sheen of smoke,
and I wanted to eat.

# American Crow

*Tecolorico michicanae*


I. *Family*


If I say my father,
a bird of prey,
married my mother
as decoration
instead of stealing
her like his father
taught him,
will my color
make sense
as North
American,
the back
of a river
sleek as a
train track
carrying the green
headdress of Montezuma
when I know it was never
made from feathers—
a relic of the Spanish
like a last name
which says we come
from here by way of water.

II. *Description*

My wings larger
than my body
brown against blue
I fly when I want to
twig in mouth I will
build a nest again
and the screech owl
will laugh and laugh.
He doesn't like my head—
too much reflection—
or my mouth
dripping with
the gold wedding
band I place above
my head.
The first bird
to love me
wrote his name
on my knuckles.
His mother watched
and nodded her head
as if I were already
owned.

III. *Range*

I hated New York
because I could
never see the moon.
There were no stars
just pigeons for me
to chase on sidewalks
their coo a reminder
of Michigan and my
family I would
return to.

IV. *Feeding Behavior*

I pack sardines in my over-
night bag, crackers,
tomato, and cucumber.
The meal my grandfather
passed down with
his wide forehead.
The delicate flip
of an egg into the hand
of a tortilla bloodied
with hot sauce.

V. *Nesting and Breeding*

I never wanted more
than an apartment
with wood floors
and a Ford Escort.

VI. *Songs and Calls*

My sound
can be misleading—
too familiar—
silver and echo
from my neck.
I cannot find
the map of iridescent
hatch marks I leave
spinning, searching,
waiting for my mother
to call me home.

# Parallel Universe

Now that the ability to have a baby is being taken away from me
I think, maybe, I would have been an ok mom until I realize
the world and how awful is it to be alive sometimes
to watch things around me destroyed or let go in the way
I will have to do, eventually with all those things I love like making
    my mother's
bed, unraveling the rosary under her pillow, placing it on her dresser,
folding her clothes the precise way she taught me, and tucking them
    into her drawer.
I will have no one to do this with me, but if I could, I wonder what it
    would be
like to share my husband's kindness or his unlimited capacity for my
    madness
because our child would think he is the tallest man alive, as I did when
I stood on my tippy toes to kiss him and thought he grew up in the
    middle of nowhere
when he told me he had to chop wood each morning to heat his
    parents' house.
He would take us up north, not as outsiders or tourists, but as a family.
    Together
we'd walk hand in hand between and against all those shores I once
    found uninviting.

# Cortés Burning the Aviaries

Last night, I let in all the birds.
I told my grandmother to stay awhile.
I said, stop disguising yourself as wind.
You are not the only one who can fly.

I told my grandmother to stay awhile.
There is something in the wind. I recognize your voice.
You are not the only one who can fly.
Have you seen Montezuma's aviaries—still green, full of breath?

There is something in the wind. I recognize your voice.
You talk to me all at once with your mouth full.
Have you seen Montezuma's aviaries—still green, full of breath?
*Cuídate*, I thought you were blessing me.

You talk to me all at once with your mouth full.
I don't believe in god but I do believe in Mexicans.
*Cuídate*, I thought you were blessing me.
I am sorry I picked all your red tulips.

I don't believe in god but I do believe in Mexicans.
I said, stop disguising yourself as wind.
I am sorry I picked all your red tulips.
Last night, I let in all the birds.

*Notes*

ANALOG is a golden shovel using "Nothing Gold Can Stay" by Robert Frost as its source text.

BIRDS OF A FEATHER borrows the structure of Deborah Paredez's "A Show of Hands."

CUTTING THE TAIL is a cento/erasure hybrid taken from Gabriel García Márquez's *One Hundred Years of Solitude*, translated by Gregory Rabassa.

EACH IS ANOTHER AND NO OTHER borrows its title from a line in "Wind, Water, Stone" by Octavio Paz and was created from a prompt from my poetry pen pal Mariya Zilberman.

FIVE THINGS BORROWED was inspired by an interview in *The Believer Magazine* between Sandra Cisneros and her translator, Liliana Valenzuela.

HAND OVER HEART is a golden shovel using The Pledge of Allegiance as its source text.

JOHN JAMES AUDUBON AND THE BATTLE OF SAN JACINTO uses research from Matthew R. Halley's "The (literal) skeletons in the closet of American Ornithology." #birdnamesforbirds

MÉXICO CITY IN THE MIDDLE OF MICHIGAN draws its inspiration from Amalia Hernández's Ballet Folklórico de México.

ORNITHOLOGY is after Theodore Roethke's "The Waking."

POEM IN CONSIDERATION OF MY DEATH is after César Vallejo's "Black Stone Lying on a White Stone."

SOY DE LA LUNA takes its title from "The Littlest Don Quixotes Versus the World" by Valeria Luiselli.

*Acknowledgments*

Thank you to the following journals where these poems were published, sometimes in slightly different forms: *Academy of American Poets Poem-a-Day, The Atlantic, Beloit Poetry Journal, Black Warrior Review, BOAAT, BreakBeat Poets vol. 4: LatiNEXT, Cleaver Magazine's Life as Activism, Cosmonauts Avenue, Ecotone, Electric Lit, Essay Daily, The Fiddlehead, Fifth Wednesday Journal, The Florida Review, Frontier Poetry, Glass: A Journal of Poetry (Poets Resist), Gastronomica, Guernica Magazine, Honey Literary, Huizache, Indiana Review, The Ilanot Review, La Libreta, Latino Book Review Magazine, The Missouri Review, the museum of americana, The Nation, Newfound, Pleiades, Poet Lore, Poetry Northwest, Porkbelly Press Myth+Magic, Rogue Agent, The Rupture, The Slowdown, Sportklet, Terrain.org, Up the Staircase Quarterly, Waxwing, Wildness,* and *Witness Magazine.*

Thank you to my creators—José & Rita Rico. And thank you to their creators—José & Nieves Rico and Eli & Mary Lapinski.

Thank you to Keith Taylor—the professor of birds.

Thank you to Professor Lisa M. Barksdale-Shaw for putting me in honors composition at Saginaw Valley State University.

Thank you to Laura Esparza who listened to and rooted for my poetry since we were children.

Thank you to Washtenaw Community College's Culinary Arts

Program. Thank you for showing me structure and that I can do anything and still be a poet.

Thank you to the Bear River Writers' Conference. Thank you to Cody Walker, Polly Rosenwaike, Laura Kasischke, Jerry Dennis, Thomas Lynch, and Richard Tillinghast. Thank you for being the best of colleagues and the greatest of friends.

Thank you to the Helen Zell Writers' Program at the University of Michigan. Thank you to my brilliant cohort and my brilliant professors—Aisha Sabatini Sloan, Susan Najita, and the one and only Diane Seuss—who saw this book in the beginning.

Thank you to Kaveh Akbar for choosing this book and thank you to Martha Rhodes, Ryan Murphy, Jonathan Blunk, and to Four Way Books for giving my book a chance to soar.

Thank you to Andrew Collard who looked at the first of these poems with gentleness.

Thank you to Ellen Stone who is the best friend and poetry pen pal a human could ask for.

Thank you to my husband, Todd Everett, for showing me Jim Harrison, the great north, sailing, the Detroit Lions, and love. You make me believe everything is possible. I adore you.

WE ARE ALSO GRATEFUL TO THOSE INDIVIDUALS WHO PARTICIPATED IN
OUR BUILD A BOOK PROGRAM. THEY ARE:

Anonymous (14), Robert Abrams, Michael Ansara, Kathy Aponick,
Michael Anna de Armas, Jean Ball, Sally Ball, Clayre Benzadón,
Adrian Blevins, Laurel Blossom, Adam Bohannon, Betsy Bonner,
Patricia Bottomley, Lee Briccetti, Joel Brouwer, Susan Buttenwieser,
Anthony Cappo, Paul and Brandy Carlson, Dan Clarke, Mark Conway,
Elinor Cramer, Kwame Dawes, John Del Peschio,
Brian Komei Dempster, Patrick Donnelly, Lynn Emanuel, Blas Falconer,
Jennifer Franklin, John Gallaher, Reginald Gibbons,
Rebecca Kaiser Gibson, Dorothy Tapper Goldman, Julia Guez,
Naomi Guttman and Jonathan Mead, Forrest Hamer, Luke Hankins,
Yona Harvey, KT Herr, Karen Hildebrand, Carlie Hoffman,
Glenna Horton, Thomas and Autumn Howard, Catherine Hoyser,
Elizabeth Jackson, Linda Susan Jackson, Jessica Jacobs and
Nickole Brown, Lee Jenkins, Elizabeth Kanell, Nancy Kassell,
Maeve Kinkead, Victoria Korth, Brett Lauer and Gretchen Scott,
Howard Levy, Owen Lewis and Susan Ennis, Margaree Little,
Sara London and Dean Albarelli, Tariq Luthun, Myra Malkin,
Louise Mathias, Victoria McCoy, Lupe Mendez, Michael and
Nancy Murphy, Kimberly Nunes, Susan Okie and Walter Weiss,
Cathy McArthur Palermo, Veronica Patterson, Jill Pearlman,
Marcia and Chris Pelletiere, Sam Perkins, Susan Peters and
Morgan Driscoll, Maya Pindyck, Megan Pinto, Kevin Prufer,
Martha Rhodes and Jean Brunel, Paula Rhodes, Louise Riemer,
Peter and Jill Schireson, Rob Schlegel, Yoana Setzer,
Soraya Shalforoosh, Mary Slechta, Diane Souvaine, Barbara Spark,
Catherine Stearns, Jacob Strautmann, Yerra Sugarman, Arthur Sze and
Carol Moldaw, Marjorie and Lew Tesser, Dorothy Thomas,
Rosalynde Vas Dias, Rushi Vyas, Martha Webster and Robert Fuentes,
Abby Wender and Rohan Weerasinghe, Rachel Weintraub and
Allston James, and Monica Youn.